Everywhere Hope

EVERYWHERE
HOPE

ENCOURAGING MOMENTS IN PROSE AND POETRY

PAULA VELOSO BABADI

XULON PRESS

Xulon Press
2301 Lucien Way #415
Maitland, FL 32751
407.339.4217
www.xulonpress.com

This book is an original work of memoir non-fiction and poetry. Names, places, events and incidents are from personal memory. They are presented through the author's filters.

Printed in the United States of America.

ISBN-13: 9781545650325

CONTENTS

INTRODUCTION

*Ask, and it will be given you; search, and
you will find; knock, and the door will be
opened for you. For everyone who asks
receives, and everyone who searches
finds, and for everyone who knocks, the
door will be opened. (Matthew 7:7-8)*

I was eight years old when I first tried to describe
hope by writing a poem during the middle of a
hurricane. Over my lifetime, I've come to realize that
to have hope you first must search, and ask, before
you receive it.

My parents, family and friends – people just like
you - nurtured hope within me, especially when I
most needed strengthening. Now, it's my turn to
give back; to share, and maybe, offer strength to
those who search.

Rejoice in hope, be patient in suffering, persevere in prayer. (Romans 12:12)

We all suffer but hope really is everywhere when we have eyes to see and hearts to believe in a fruitful harvest.

Life's unexpected occurrences provide a rich field for growing and reaping harvests, despite plagues and pestilence. This collection celebrates hope that arises from facing everyday challenges, with eyes fixed on the One who made us. This is for you.

For everything that was written in the past was written to teach us, so that through the endurance taught in the Scriptures and the encouragement they provide we might have hope. (Romans 15:4)

CHAPTER 1:

CHILDREN

*I*was a difficult child, willful and stubborn, but somehow my devoted parents made it through the tantrums and drama.** Now, I have four grown children and three grandchildren. Over the years, I've made many mistakes. The one thing I've learned is that love is what counts the most. You can't go wrong when you love genuinely.

> *Above all, maintain constant love for one another, for love covers a multitude of sins. (1Peter 4:8)*

About Rainbows

When I bring clouds over the earth and the bow is seen in the clouds, I will remember my covenant which is between me and you and every living creature of all flesh; and the waters shall never again become a flood to destroy all flesh. (Genesis 9:14-15)

When I was a young mother, I lost patience, after a long day at the hospital, when my two-year-old son wouldn't quit hanging on my leg. I was happy to see him, but all I could think of was changing my clothes and getting out of my nursing shoes.

The moment I snapped at him, I wanted to take back those sharp words. He was wounded. Immediately, I regretted my tone of voice. Clinging to me was his way of showing he loved and missed me. The incident negatively impacted me just as much as it hurt him. I had trouble coping with my feelings – what mother rejects her toddler? I got through that trauma by remembering the promise of rainbows.

About Rainbows

Your tiny lip quivers
like a fragile leaf
insulted by the weight of a raindrop,
until the tears come –
violently and uncontrolled
like the storm's torrent.

If only you could hear me
through the thunder of your cry –
I could tell you that I know;
that the sharp flick of lightening goes fast away;
that I am sorry my cloud
happened to rain on you.

Instead, my arms reach out –
their friendly sky enfolding you.
And I thank God
that sunshine's warmth can melt away
the bitterness of words spat out
like hard, cold rain.

Your lip blossoms into a flower-smile,
(but my heart aches over all the storms
you will ever know)
and I just hold you closer
to tell you about rainbows.

ROSEMARY

Train children in the right way, and when
old, they will not stray. (Proverbs 22:6)

O ne year, I had two beautifully shaped rose-
mary topiaries. I delighted to be around them
while taking in the intense fragrance. Rosemary has
a rich history and multitude of uses beyond food
flavoring and medicine. It is down to earth, but topi-
aries require planning, precision, and persistent
care to get to the desired form. I gave up on taming
them. As a result, I discovered trailing Rosemary

spreads freely and cascades over its pot. It is happy just being Rosemary and not conforming to a pre-determined shape.

I learned to love watching how it takes on a life of its own and am content to clip here, and there, once in a while as a loving gardener does; otherwise letting it grow as it will. Whether it is neatly trimmed and shaped, or trailing along a wall, its essence doesn't change.

Watching Rosemary, trimmed and untrimmed, helped me understand my youngest son, at a time when he sought to reach beyond the confines of neat and tidy pots at home to wander across the unknown paths ahead.

Rosemary

Simple,

yet complex,

polished yet wild,

intense and down to

earth, "dew of the sea."

The stuff of legend,

rich with history and ripe

with myriad medicinal magic;

no neatly clipped topiary

trailing over the pot's rim

seeking freedom while roots

well grounded, harbour within

familiar walls. Sharp needles belie

the flower, tough branches never tell

the tale of clippings sowing subtle flavor

in the stew.

He is beloved

my rosemary son.

HER PRAYERS

He called a little child to him and placed the child among them. And he said: "Truly I tell you, unless you change and become like little children, you will never enter the kingdom of heaven. Therefore, whoever takes the lowly position of this child is the greatest in the kingdom of heaven. (Matthew 18:2-4).

By the time my youngest child was five, I was worn out from work and twenty-seven years of marriage, which included multiple extended family members living with us most of that time. I began to wonder what life is about, as I tried to juggle home, work, relationships, and endless activities.

Sometimes there are deserts in the richness and blessings of family and work life. I faithfully went to church, prayed, and tried to find balance through it all. I found myself thirsting for something more, during a period of dryness, when I couldn't see the palm trees or oases right in front of me.

One evening, God reminded me of his nearness and care as I witnessed my daughter saying her nightly prayers. The experience was everything I needed. To this day, that scene remains with me, a testament to the soothing love of my heavenly Father.

Her Prayers

With small hands folded
and head bowed earnestly,
her clear, sweet voice implores.

She talks to God with innocence and trust,
no doubt of an answer –
just a simple knowing that her Friend will hear.

And when her words wash over me
like new spring rains,
they quench the parched desert of my soul
and I am, for a moment, removed
from raging storms and burning sands
to rest in the oasis of pure and soothing love.

I thank God for rescue in the rising of her prayers.

CHILD'S TEARS

Lord, you have probed me, you know me: you know when I sit and stand; you understand my thoughts from afar. You sift through my travels and my rest; with all my ways you are familiar. Even before a word is on my tongue, LORD, you know it all.(Psalm 139:1-4)

C anyons are formed from years of erosion that result in a narrow path, where water cut between the high, surrounding walls. They are deep. In exreme contrast, a puddle after a rainshower is shallow. The same holds true of wounds.

A child's grief over a fallen ice-cream cone might easily be remedied by another cone. But the grief of being misunderstood, or not accepted, requires a greater remedy.

God knows us to our core. He understands us and accepts us. When fellow human beings misunderstand me, or wrongly interpret my actions, it is enough to know the Lord gets me. I can let go.

That wasn't always true for me. I allowed what people thought, or said about me, to cause me pain; cause my tears to flow. I've been accused of crying child's tears. Even if I could find the words to correct misconceptions, there was never the guarantee of a receptive ear – except for the Lord.

A wonderful priest told me how much God loves me and advised I memorize Psalm 139 – a way to remember. I typed it up and have now carried it around with me for years. The psalmist continues:

You formed my inmost being; you knit me in my mother's womb. I praise you, because I am wonderfully made; wonderful are your works! My very self you know. My bones are not hidden from you, when I was being made in secret, fashioned in the depths of the earth. (Psalm 139:13-15)

When no one on this earth really knows – He does. And in the deep canyon wound, along with tears, there is beauty and release.

Child's Tears

Shallow?

Child's tears
grieving fallen ice-cream cones?

NO!

Unspoken answers make pictures
incomplete.
Puzzles are un-pieceable.

Weeping springs from canyon wounds,
Until I remember You know me.

Chapter 2:

RELATIONSHIPS

I'm still working on who I want to be when I
grow up. While I'm still working on the details,
one thing I am sure of is that who I want to be is
someone filled with love – for God and for all his
children – the body of Christ.

At the heart of love is relationship, and relation-
ships are sometimes the hardest challenge for me.

> *He answered, "You shall love the Lord*
> *your God with all your heart, and with*
> *all your soul, and with all your strength,*
> *and with all your mind; and your*
> *neighbor as yourself." (Luke 10:27)*

No Stone for David

*The islanders showed us unusual kind-
ness. They built a fire and welcomed
us all because it was raining and cold.
(Acts 28:2)*

I believe every aspect of God's created world pro-
vides an opportunity for us to find Him. Even

the pouring rain, cold and stinging as it may be, confirmed the goodness and kindness of my fellow man – a reflection of God's care for every detail of our lives.

This is a tribute to David, a co-worker, who got soaking wet making sure I stayed dry during a period of recuperation from knee surgery. He battled the angry sky, from our work building to my car, beat the giant and won my sincerest appreciation.

No Stone for David

Today, open sky
pouring Goliath tears
straight-aimed at naked places
vulnerable
to the sea outside,
pelts harder than the ancient shepherd's stone.

This day,

no stone for David to slay lion or bear

in rescue of his father's sheep,

just a heart

expanding larger than the giant,

pulsing quicker than a slingshot

in a breath

without thought for self,

whose kindness saved me.

No stone for you, David

against the angry sky –

only a simple umbrella

offered by your warm heart

to this thankful soul.

SHE COULD HAVE BEEN A DUCHESS

*I thank my God every time I remember
you. (Philippians 1:3)*

My oldest son was recently in London when
he called to ask the address of my child-
hood home. He was surprised when I rattled it off
zip code and all. When he found the location, Jahan

took a picture of the three-story row home at 9 New Kings Road, Fulham, London, S.W. 6 – once home to William and Edith Pumfrey, my mother's parents – my beloved Nanny and Grandpa. We lived with them when my father was out at sea, until we moved into another childhood home on Epple Road.

It was easy for me to remember my grandparents' address because at age eight, when we moved to America, I wrote letters to Nanny and Grandpa all the time. They responded, each writing in their own hand on the thin blue air mail letter paper rarely seen these days. Grandpa had beautiful penmanship, grand enough to grace a scroll with his English script. He wrote to me in rhymes and I still have those letters today, over fifty years later, tucked away in my letter tin. Nanny's penmanship on the other hand was often difficult to read, but her letters were just as eagerly anticipated as those of my grandfather.

Writing back and forth with both of them created a treasured bond that the thousand-mile distance could never break. My grandparents were an important part of my life. So, when Jahan sent me pictures, I was overjoyed. I remembered looking out of my third story bedroom window in the mornings listening to the sound of London waking up.

Back then, we still had horse drawn milk wagons and coal deliveries amidst the honking horns and red double decker buses. I imagined what it might be like if our family had kept 9 New Kings Road.

The home was empty at the time I wrote this memory. My son relayed it was up for sale in Fulham's historic district for several million pounds sterling! It may be worth millions of dollars, but there is no price that can match the treasured childhood memories I have when we lived with my grandparents and corresponded over the years.

She Could Have Been a Duchess
(for Edith Pumfrey)

She could have been a duchess –
crocheted silk turban
neatly broached
at the center seam,
tortoise shell cigarette holder
sporting an unfiltered smoke
in perfect lips framed with
peaches and cream soft skin.

She didn't pencil in the mole
cornering her smiling mouth,
it was her own mark
signaling her beauty
more than the fashionable hats
she wore and loved.
She laughed a lot.
Plump and stubborn,
she wore short neat wigs
when turban or hat
was not her fancy.

Green was her favorite colour;
she loved Tom Jones
and Englebert Humberdinck,
baked rice pudding in
white porcelain clad pans,
and gathered us for afternoon tea
with dainty buttered cucumber sandwiches
or sometimes,
fish paste and Marmite.

She was the most glamorous person
I knew back then
sending packages of
"mod" dainties across the Atlantic
in tissue-papered boxes
from Selfridges
accompanied by thin blue
aero-mail letters penned with a
nearly hieroglyphic hand.

She could have been a duchess –
this Welsh coal miner's daughter,
orphaned at three,
tenderness toughened
from years of boarding school
afforded by her kindly
tea-magnate uncle-
almost disinherited
when she wed
her blue-eyed blond
pure Anglo-Saxon commoner
for love.

She could have been a duchess but
she was so much more to me.

BUILDING CASTLES

Bear with each other and forgive one another if any of you has a grievance against someone. Forgive as the Lord forgave you. And over all these virtues put on love, which binds them all together in perfect unity. Let the peace of Christ rule in your hearts, since as members of one body you were called to peace. And be thankful. (Colossians 3: 13-15)

G oing to the beach was a big part of family life growing up in Pensacola. We spent many occasions picnicking on the deserted shores of the pristine Gulf. Our Sunday ritual was Morning Mass, then treks beyond the dunes to immerse ourselves in clear emerald waters. We drank in sun, surf and sand before anyone ever heard of skin cancer or sunscreen.

Once I married and moved away from home, I forgot for a while about those languid days. In the hub bub of starting my own family, I grew apart from the family of my childhood. Months turned into years until I began to feel that the gulf between us was too great to cross. We drifted apart and stayed that way for about ten years.

After my years of silence, and sadness at missing my childhood family, one day at Mass, the Holy Spirit soothed my longing soul with words that brought back remembered love.

I scribbled thoughts in the margins of the bulletin and cried tears of thanksgiving at Holy Communion for the hope welling inside. I contacted my parents and gave them this poem. We reconciled and have remained close ever since.

Building Castles

We built castles in the sand
When I was very young
And secured them with our laughter
Under rays of warming sun.

But changing tides did batter
Against our castle walls
Eroding them to ruins
Frail and small.

Now nightfall after nightfall
Countless tides have played their hand
And castles we once fashioned
Are lost beneath the sand.

I'm no longer shedding tears
Because I've come to know
The castles from my childhood
Are everywhere I go.

This gentle truth fell over me
Like a wave from God above-
The castles etched within my heart
Were always built with love.

ACCEPTING ONIONS

For if their rejection is the reconciliation of the world, what will their acceptance be but life from the dead! (Romans 11:15)

I am continually amazed at how much wisdom can be imparted from God's green earth. Take the onion – just as it comes to us from the ground, the onion is at once, intense, pungent and strong, yet so readily torn when we handle the delicate skin and made sweet when sautéed. Scientists have tried to suppress the onion enzyme that causes us to cry, but in doing so, they discovered their engineering caused unwanted changes in the onion's essence and compromised its health benefits.

Something as simple as an onion contains contradictions. I decided to accept it for what it is, as it is, without alteration; to enjoy raw tears along with delectable taste. My husband and I laugh, because I call him my onion and wrote this poem about our relationship. We've been through the raw, sweet and savory times. You know what I mean. I love onions, but they still make me cry, now and then, when I forget the secrets that can halt tears.

God, in His infinite wisdom, provides us with paradoxes in the "whole" of this created world and in His children. My prayer to our heavenly Father today is one of thanksgiving for opening my eyes to see and appreciate the mysteries of this earth applied to our humanity, especially my own "onion."

<u>Accepting Onions</u>

I'm an onion through and through
You like me when I'm in the stew,
Flavor mingling with the rest
I think that's when you like me best.
When you face me raw I make you cry
My taste too strong for you to try,
But persevere and you will find
The secrets in each layer of mine –
For though my flavor is intense
My benefits are quite immense.
Polyphenols, flavenoids,
Boost the heart, fill diet voids.
They reside in my first layer
So peel me with the greatest care.
Anti-bacterial, good with liver,
Even helps with the blood sugar.
To get these benefits you must commit
To take me daily and never quit.
Don't like onions? Think again,
I give you paper from my skin.
Pungent taste enjoyed through time
I'm the star of feta, pita, herbs and wine.

33

Those who've learned to appreciate me
Discovered there's more than what they see.
I know I'm harsh, and sometimes rotten, then
You throw me out, completely forgotten.
But I'm also tasty, savory, and sweet
The choice is yours, whether or not to eat.
And when my panthial S-Oxide makes you cry
Remember my qualities that elicit a sigh.
I may be just your onion,
In some ways good and some not,
But without you to complete me,
I'm only food in the pot.
It's when you accept me for what I am,
I become the finest pick of the land.

CARDINAL RED

You know that you were ransomed from the futile ways inherited from your ancestors, not with perishable things like silver or gold, but with the precious blood of Christ, like that of a lamb without defect or blemish. (1 Peter 1:18-19)

Advent and Christmas were always bright and happy times in my childhood home. While focus was on preparing for the coming of Christ, mixed in with that anticipation was the fun of decorating. Red was everywhere, in every room. My mother made sure our home reflected the joy heralded by the angels, with the manger scene as a focal point. We had red plaid table cloths in the dining room and playful elves hanging from every conceivable perch. I came to love the significance of all these bright red decorations.

Several years ago, a cardinal perched outside my window one morning. He was a magnificent red contrast against the small oak tree in my backyard. His presence reminded me of my father, who faithfully put out black sunflower seeds (the best kind) for the cardinals gracing our home.

My mother keeps a stained-glass cardinal on her bedroom window along with a myriad of colored-glass crucifixes, chalices, and other professions of her enduring faith. She believes that my dad, long gone, signals to her when the cardinals come and visit.

So, my mind wandered from Advent and Christmas, filled with red decorations, to the red of the cardinal. I find it amazing how much the color red permeates our world, and how God created so many variations for our delight. I reflected upon the fact that it was the deep scarlet of the cardinal that is reminiscent of our Savior; not at His birth but at His redemptive sacrifice. In my reflection, one thing was crystal clear to me, one realization that I needed at the time; Jesus loves me. He loves all of us, beyond our imagining, beyond all else in this created world. I marvel at God's wisdom in creating a small bird with such power to move the human heart, to lift my spirits toward heaven, and to give me memories of my devout parents.

The following poem was born from the gift of red given to me through inspiring parents. What memories bring warmth and comfort to you?

Cardinal Red

More than poinsettias or
red curly-ribboned Christmas gifts,
more than glossy lacquered lines
of red candy apples in the window,
more than clumsy Crayola-red shapes
on a toddler's first piece of art,
more than sumptuous strawberry-red berries
begging to be tasted,
more than the competent clarity of fire engine reds
racing to rescue,

the deep scarlet cardinal captures me
in the fleeting seconds of his landing,
in the sound of his call,
in the almost imperceptible rising and falling
of his splendid chest.

He breathes life and bleeds red,
as red as the drops of blood
falling from our Savior's wounds,
and causes me to remember my father
quoting Matthew 6:26 from his red Douay-Rheims

"Behold the birds of the air, for they neither sow,

nor do they reap, nor gather into barns;

and your heavenly Father feedeth them.

Are not you of much more value than they?"

In this cardinal red moment,

the two hundred and eighty-four other shades

referenced in books

cannot compare.

PRAYER BLANKET

Because there is one bread, we who are
many are one body, for we all partake
of the one bread. (1 Corinthians 10:17)

One November, when I mentioned that I would not be attending a Hearts Afire retreat session due to upcoming surgery, one of my sisters in Christ, Sheila, brought me a prayer blanket. We were at Mass, and I cried when she gave it to me. She said it was from the whole group. I had heard about the Covered in Prayer ministry, but really didn't know much about it. As soon as I was able to place the perfectly colored and patterned blanket over me and say the prayers, I could feel the love, warmth, compassion, and blessings conveyed in the very fabric that comforted my welcoming shoulders.

To understand the enormity of what getting this blanket meant, you need to know that many years ago after attending a Christ Renews His Parish retreat weekend (CRHP), I gave a witness to the next CRHP group on Christian Community. For most of my life, I practiced my faith devoutly and quietly, in the background and outskirts of parish life, alone. CRHP was the beginning of my journey to outwardly participating in the community, the body of Christ. I progressed over the years to engaging in church life, when I was able. Receiving that blanket signified externally that I was, and am, part of the Christian community.

The story doesn't end there. I was so taken by this gift, so comforted, that I hurriedly made a prayer blanket to give to my Mother for her birthday. I brought it with me to Pensacola before it could be prayed over by the People of Praise, on Tuesday, or blessed during the Wednesday Mass with all the other blankets. My Mum had never heard of a prayer blanket before and I explained what had happened to me and how I wanted her to have one too. After I came home from work at the Pensacola office one day, she gave it back to me letting me know how nice it was, but she wanted the prayers, blessings and Mass that came along with it. Of course, I totally agreed to make sure the blanket went through the proper process.

I brought the blanket home with me and Sue, from the Hearts Afire group, took it to have it prayed over, blessed and returned to me at our next group retreat session. I sent the blanket back to my mother along with the envelope of prayers, readings and rosary. To my delight, I got a phone call late one evening. Mum had received her prayer blanket that day, used it and couldn't wait to tell me how she immediately felt the difference in her blanket after it truly was "Covered in Prayer."

It became so clear to me then, how the body of Christ extends far beyond local parish life. My Catholic faith creates a communion among believers, as well as a comfort and belonging that comes with being part of the body of Christ, no matter our physical location. "Though we are many parts, we are all one body..." (Romans 12:5) is a living testament of truth.

Prayer Blanket

Fibers filled

With the Father's fervent love

Shaped through the Spirit

Made whole because of the Son

Pressed together and spread

By the Body of Christ

Warm us,

Heal us,

Cover us.

SWEET LIGHT

God made the two great lights—the greater light to rule the day and the lesser light to rule the night—and the stars. (Genesis 1:16)

After forty three years of marriage - blissful blue skies, thunderous storms and haphazard hurricanes, I have come to a place of peace and rest in the magical twilight that photographers call "sweet." With all the ups and downs that inevitably occur in such a long relationship, it is a wonderful realization that my husband and I can share our golden years in this "blue hour."

It hasn't always been easy and getting to this place required a lot of hard work on both our parts. My husband is outgoing, charismatic, outspoken and opinionated. I can be stubborn and opinionated, but essentially, I am an introvert. We seem to be opposites, as I let him shine when we are out together, while I linger in the background.

I am reminded of Jeff Silbar and Larry Henley's song popularized by the likes of Bette Midler and Celene Dion, "Wind Beneath My Wings," and I am content. God created night and day, each with its own wonders. It's OK to be in the shadow of night, because inevitably, the two are joined as one, and that is enough for me.

<u>Sweet Light</u>

No shadows here when light is
"L'Heure Bleue" to artist eyes
or "sweet" to camera canvas.
One side of earth
basks in your sunlight
while I rest shadowed
on the other side.

You are brilliant day
burning, tumultuous, blinding, busy, wide awake.
I am subdued night
serene, quiescent, muted, dreaming, slumbering.
You own most phases of the earth's turning as
your searing light often blinds onlookers
to the pale beauty behind your blaze.
My light reflects gently on the quieter side where,

when you're gone, the stars become visible.

Our co-existence is casually questionable
and yet, for all our differences,
we twice share Twilight
when earth succumbs to neither night nor day.
In the blue hour of this sweet light, we are one.
It is enough for me.

46

Chapter 3:

MERCY

Blessed are the merciful, for they will receive mercy. (Matthew 5:7)

We are called to be merciful, so that we might receive mercy.** I admit this is a hard one. I admire and strive to be like those who exemplify mercy and forgiveness. Jesus gave us the greatest example of mercy and forgiveness when he hung on the cross. God's mercy toward me has been lifesaving. I have a long way to go in this respect, but I continually try. When I read about people like Immaculee LLibagiza of Rwanda, author of *Left to Tell,* [1] I marvel at her capacity for mercy and forgiveness and only hope one day, I might have her capacity. For now, I rely fully on God's mercy.

By the tender mercy of our God, the dawn from on high will break upon us. (Luke 1:78)

CONFESSION

*If we confess our sins, he who is faithful
and just will forgive us our sins and
cleanse us from all unrighteousness.
(1 John 1:9)*

Most of my life, I viewed Confession as a bur-
densome part of being Catholic. I dreaded
going. Facing the priest with the same sins again,
and again, or giving voice to any sin at all, felt awful.
But a simple incident reminded me of a key life

lesson–we fear what we don't truly know, or understand, and Jesus always removes that fear.

When one of my sons moved back home with his American Pit Bull Terrier, I was mildly fearful around her. Dallas had an imposing frame and thickly-muscled broad head. One day, as I came through the front door, tired from a long work day, Dallas greeted me with bared teeth and heavy breathing, back and forth, through her menacing canines. Unsure, I stood near the door calling for my son. Daniel laughed when he saw me standing, briefcase still in hand, with Dallas "smiling" and eager for me to greet her. My son explained she was not baring her teeth to scare me; she was smiling because I was part of her pack and she was happy to see me.

With Daniel close by, I stooped down and grinned back at Dallas, pushing air back and forth through my teeth following her enthusiastic example. Her tail gyrated at hurricane force. I never feared Dallas again. Once I understood her intent, we "smiled" at each other on a regular basis. We became friends.

I do not tell the story of a menacing dog, with bared teeth, to mean it is the same as facing a priest in the confessional. Rather, I share this story to illustrate a point. Once I understood what was really going on with Dallas, fear left me.

Gaining a better understanding of confession made a difference in my life, too. Growing up I knew confession was good for me, but I was fearful. I knew it provided sacramental grace by lifting the burden of guilt from my soul, yet the dread persisted. Through a parish retreat program, Hearts Afire, fear *really* left me. At last, I understood confession as Jesus' intense longing for friendship and union with us –his body, the branches of his vine. Jesus is rooted and waiting at the threshold to embrace, forgive, love, console, and commune with us–with me!

It's been a journey to embrace confession and appreciate Our Lord's wisdom in this sacramental gift. Retreat materials from Father Michael Gaitley, MIC so beautifully state,

> *"Wonder of wonders" Jesus remains truly with us, not just in our minds through his Word, not just in our souls through faith and grace, but also* bodily

present with us in his Sacraments, where he continues to bless, forgive, cleanse, unite, heal, strengthen and make all things new. [2]

Just as understanding Dallas' intense greeting allayed my fears, understanding Jesus' intention for us through the miraculous sacrament of Confession changed me. While I don't pretend to understand it all, I know in my heart that Jesus gave us confession as a means for us to grow closer to Him, to keep getting up from the depths of the fall and continue reaching upward toward His light. Confession is still a bit uncomfortable for me. But I know Jesus' ocean of mercy covers all. And for the repentant heart, then comes intimate communion, through Jesus, with God, by the loving bond of the Holy Spirit.

Confession

In sunless depths, my wreckage

In darkness lies

In cold silence

In suppressed screams

Scattered below the sandy floor.

Metal hull

Hides from sonar waves

Skeletal remnants,

Sins buried beneath

Photosynthesis reach.

I have evaded anchor's curves

Trolling lines

Rescue from tumult

Light's warmth

Long enough.

"Bless me father, for I have sinned,"

 It seems an eternity since my last confession

"And these are my sins."

 His mercy is an ocean.

His light pierces darkness
His love reaches down,
Pulls me to his arms
Where I rest inside His heart.

"O my God, I am heartily sorry for having
offended thee."
His mercy is an ocean
Offering respite on glassy surfaces
Reflecting sky of balmy summer days
Beckoning upward a true and steady course
Back to the sun,
Promising purity
And peace that
Once I knew.

GEODE'S ODE

Therefore, judge nothing before the appointed time; wait until the Lord comes. He will bring to light what is hidden in darkness and will expose the motives of the heart. At that time each will receive their praise from God. (1 Corinthians 4:5)

One day, during my career, I felt passed over and drab, as younger, and prettier co-workers caught the attention of leaders in our division. Besides being older, I was obviously overweight. Although I always dressed for the job I wanted and had valuable experience gained from years of hard work, I felt sorry for myself- I bought a wig. I thought I was like a geode; those dull rocks in geology kits with rough, dark exteriors that go unappreciated, until broken in half to reveal unique, colorful insides.

By the time the weekend rolled around, out of curiosity, I Googled "geode" and what I found took my breath away! It testified to God's splendor. How could something so beautiful be hidden away beneath a dark shell? I had to know more and spent my entire Saturday reading about these marvels – how they begin, their formation, their arrival at the place that makes them what they are.

It became apparent to me that human beings, God's most majestic creation, take somewhat the same journey as the geode. It's the struggle, the adversity, the pressure and our reactions which create our unique beauty – sometimes hidden from our own eyes, but present and always noticed by our Creator. I am ever thankful, that in His goodness and wisdom, He sends people into our lives to help us see as He sees; my wig now resides, forgotten, at the back of a dresser drawer.

I identified with the Geode's formation, but there was one fact that jumped out at me. When the volcanic bubbles that are often caught inside the core of the geode finally burst, they leave a small space at the center of the rock. It remains unfilled. I began to think of how we yearn to be complete and how we find that completeness only in our Creator. By the end of that weekend, I didn't care how anyone at work viewed me, because I knew how God saw me.

He sees all of us and knows us. We can rest assured, in Him, knowing that we are wonderfully made. Just break open a geode to see what I mean!

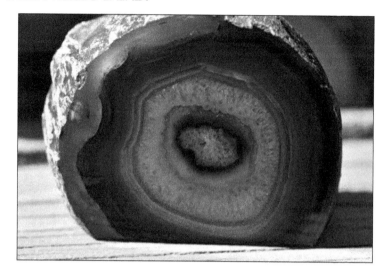

Geode's Ode

My plain, dark veneer deceives even sincere eyes
scouring rocks housing spheroids and ovoids;
contemplating what might lie beneath the surface.

I am formed from harsh erosion, unmerciful ele-
ments, transported by wind and water to the place
where you find me.
But I was born innocent, light as a bubble
resting in the calm space beyond vol-
canic eruption
or crushed fragments from the sea.

Time hardened my shell, protecting
the empty space where bubbles burst.
Mineral–laced water seeped through rock pores,
painting me layer by layer,
depositing rich hues with each changing rain.

Your eyes could not see the pressure then,
locking me in bedrock,
pressing, squeezing, forcing each fine line to
cling within,
smooth and course – chemical colored gifts from
the ground.

My insides are organized from chaos;
orchestrated, uniquely different- drawn
portraiture
fingered by my response to nature's mighty hand.
How could you know at my core
there might still be
a small empty space
waiting to be filled,
yearning for completion so intensely that the
entire universe cannot finish it, cannot feed it,
cannot press it further –
only the Mighty Hand can do that.

Today, your eyes found me.

They were not deceived by dark, rough edges,

or incomplete formations.

Your knowing eyes and wise hand picked me up,

broke me open and showed me

the beauty God has always seen.

FALLING UPWARDS

...but those who wait for the Lord shall renew their strength, they shall mount up with wings like eagles, they shall run and not be weary, they shall walk and not faint. (Isaiah 40:31)

I never thought it would happen to me. I knew it was common, but I thought I was safe, until the day our work team was advised that three of the five project managers under our beloved "boss" were being displaced. No one wanted to leave. Over the years, we formed a tightly knit group of high performers focused on saving costs for the company, driven to excellence by the thought of making a difference, and encouraged by a leader with passion and a big heart.

God is so good though. He spared me in several ways; first by providing a fun respite, second by affording me a compassionate leader, and third, but not least, by showering me with his infinite mercy and love; a saving grace during those uncertain days.

I was shielded from the initial jolt received by my team-mates, because of an escape on a magical, serendipitous getaway before I got the news. Our team was scheduled to meet with the VP, our boss's boss on Thursday afternoon. It so happened, Thursday morning on my way to work, my daughter-in-law asked me if I wanted to fill a last minute vacant spot in her mother's cruise cabin. Of course, the possibility was off my radar. I had vendor meetings, conference calls and presentations to complete on Thursday and Friday.

As I headed for work and my first conference call for the day, second thoughts swirled in my mind. Somewhere in the five minutes between that call ending and my next meeting, I dashed into my boss's office and told her about the random offer. She looked at me and said, "If it were me, I'd find a way to rearrange my schedule and I'd go!" Enough said, I dashed to my next meeting and began looking at my calendar to plan who could cover for me and what could I re-schedule.

By ten that morning, I had a plan. I called my son, told him to call the cruise line, add my name and don't leave without me. Thirty minutes later, my vacation days were approved, my calendar cleared, and my critical meetings covered by willing friends. By noon, I was home throwing together my required medical gear, bare bones wardrobe, and basic shoes. And by two, my son, daughter-in-law, grandchildren and "Mimi", their other grandmother, hustled through check-in on our way to four days of sea and Bahama island relaxation.

On that short vacation, God provided me the joy of living in the present moment. Playing "Connect Four" with my grandsons, JJ and Behn, I thought of nothing else but them; reveling in their boyish chatter and laughter. Drinking in the color and beauty at the on-board artwork auctions, I was breathless because of colorful paintings and prints that dilated my pupils and warmed my veins. Enjoying "Mimi" playing bingo for the first time in her life, and winning, kept any thoughts of work-life in the distant past. In his mercy and love, God knew what I needed to get me past falling down, and onward, to rising upward.

Falling Upwards

Does the dandelion tuft
Mourn its wrenching from the globe
Home no longer with the rest
Curse cruel gales
Or
Ride the crest?

Do falling leaves to mulch or mold
Cry fallen hopes in season's cold
Give up their role in nature's quest
Or
Change to bedding for a nest?

Does a severed branch downed by wind
Give up its soul, its life rescind
When circumstance would name it "broke"
Or
Does it rise anew as smoke?

In the wrenching and the falling
In the severing and the breaking
In the dying

Is awakening.

Through Him

In Him

And with Him

Falling upwards.

LORD, LORD

I do not understand what I do. For what
I want to do, I do not do, but what I hate,
I do. (Romans 7:15)

God's creation contains darkness, along with light. It is a reality we cannot escape, but He provides us with the means to get through desolation and darkness– we have only to act. When night falls, we turn on a lamp; when storms rage, we run to safe shelter; when rain pelts, we raise umbrellas.

Taking action though, is not always as easy when the darkness resides within us; when we don't even recognize what danger looms in our inmost being. Where nature is honest and truthful, our fallen selves are easily deceived.

Through the darkness, God longs to carry us to dawn, but He is not forceful in His love and longing; He gives us free will. So, the one ingredient that may save us from nature's calamities is the same ingredient that saves us from ourselves – action. When we make even the slightest movement toward God's rescue, He is waiting to lift us into His loving arms.

This is a tough reality, applied to my own life. God's mercy and love are evident in my lengthy struggle with addiction to food. It's a hard topic to discuss, so I haven't talked about it for a long time, although its consequences are blatantly obvious. It's still a struggle, just like Paul's lament, but I find comfort in reaching out to the Lord. When I do, He always answers in that moment.

No matter the struggle, we can always hope in the assurance of God's mercy when we call out to Him.

Lord, Lord

I cry "Lord, Lord,"
yet stubbornly cling to the darkness of
my false god
and yield to familiar enveloping numbness.
It placates and buffers the gnawing
from which I am unwilling to reach up and
grasp the Hand
that longs to save me from myself.
I hide from the ugliness I might discover
in the light of a clear mind.
Instead, I remain dazed
from the fleeting pleasure of sweet deceits, and
fall into the pocket of oblivion where
nothing matters
any more.
What makes me think I will magically say "Yes" to
Truth that longs to find me
after a lifetime of submitting to the subtle
and easy lie?
My actions betray my heart.
It is not enough to cry "Lord, Lord."
I am convicted by Paul's lament.

If I sincerely ask for rescue, He will come
and sweep me upward.
Jesus, I trust in You.
"Lord, Lord,"
give me the strength not just to ask and trust,
but to act.

Chapter 4:

HEALING & REPAIR

*He heals the brokenhearted and binds
up their wounds. (Psalm 147:3)*

*M**y mother loves the Psalms.** I never real-
ized until much later in life what richness,
consolation and beauty they contain. Now that I'm
older, I can honestly say I have been broken count-
less times and been healed just as many.

Because I passed the first half century of my
life, I have much to share about being broken and
repaired. It didn't feel great being broken, but I
learned so much about God's love, mercy and care
for me during the healing process. This chapter
might seem sad, but in the end, it really heralds
hope. I pray you find hope and healing as I did.

"Grant me, O Lord my God,

a mind to know You,

a heart to seek You,

wisdom to find You,

conduct pleasing to You,

faithful perseverance in

waiting for You,

and a hope of finally

embracing You.

Amen."

Thomas Aquinas [3]

BROKEN SHELLS

The Lord is near to the brokenhearted
and saves the crushed in spirit.

(Psalm 34:18)

One December, when my two eldest sons were ten and five, our family enjoyed lunch at the pastel peach home of my husband's friend, nestled on the shores of Ponte Vedra Beach. As my young sons ran off looking for sharks' teeth and my husband engaged in "man-talk," I strolled the sands beyond the graceful white-paned French doors, opening to the ocean.

Amid inhaling the crisp, salty air and reveling in the more-than-cool breeze, I felt a twinge of sadness at the broad expanse of broken shells before me. How much we human beings are like these shells – huddled together, separate, yet one on the canvas of creation.

Today, along miles of shoreline, there still are jewels brushed and polished by the repeated breaking of waves and warmed to a glow by sunshine on clear (and even cloudy) days. The sun and waves unite this array, working together to paint God's unique landscape.

That day I felt broken inside, just like the shells. But, as the sun warmed my arms, I knelt to take a closer look. Our wise Creator gifted me with the hope of repurpose and repair, and the vision of being whole in Him. Whether crushed or damaged, we are part of His perfect painting; His masterpiece. That vision gives me hope.

Broken Shells

Broken shells upon the shore
washed in by gentle waves once more,
paint the sand with shattered dreams –
their beauty lost in fragments.

One masterpiece in the array,
amidst the broken pieces lay
too well concealed for me to see
its beauty on the canvas.

Though I am broken-pieced this day,
God's healing sun and ocean spray
brush me into a form anew
whole again amidst the broken shells.

CITRUS BLUES

Why, my soul, are you downcast? Why so disturbed within me? Put your hope in God, for I will yet praise him, my Savior and my God. (Psalm 42:6)

Compost piles are not a pretty sight when being newly formed. They smell bad. But, as time passes, and the garbage piles up, heat and air and other matter work their magic to change it to a rich, black sweet-smelling substance that provides nourishment for other plant life to grow. But while it's in the process, it is smelly and messy and requires upkeep.

Ever feel like life is like one continual new compost pile? I have. I was a full time working mother, with two young children, married to a husband who frequently worked away from home, for long periods of time overseas. I felt sorry for myself, submerged in life's messy refuse. I had too much work, and not enough time. I was tired, wondering when the much-needed relief would come. I was at my desk, crying.

God gave me the relief I sought, while eating an orange for lunch. As I peeled and cleaned the segments of connective threads and pith, I was reminded of a universal truth, and came to believe that in the end the peel and seeds are not garbage. The orange was sweet as I bit into each piece. And as the juice exploded in my mouth, I swallowed the sweet with my bitter-blue feelings. The peel and seeds became heralds of better things to come.

And he who sat upon the throne said,
"Behold, I make all things new." Also, he

said, "Write this, for these words are
trustworthy and true." (Revelation 21:5)

Citrus Blues

Beyond the wax-like skin,

behind the rind,

beneath connective fibers,

each cell within the whole

bleeds one by one into invading atmosphere.

Dissected now,

each segment swallowed by the cavern

cries its essence bittersweet

into the void.

Peelings and pulp discarded

and undigested seeds

(food for the worms)

shall one day make a flower grow.

HINDS FEET HOPES

God, the Lord, is my strength; He makes my feet like the feet of a deer and makes me tread upon the heights. (Habakkuk 3:19)

When I was visiting the small mountain village of Miyancoo in Khuzestan, Iran, I explored the local terrain with my husband's nieces and nephews. I never saw a mountain deer, but I did see goats traipsing on the narrowest of ledges. It seemed an effortless trek for them. Was it an inborn ability, or were they guided as young kids on how to navigate the way? Mountain goats have hard outer hooves, allowing them to dig into ledges coupled with soft hoof pads that act like climbing shoes. Their bodies are physically equipped to help them traverse the trail.

Human beings are equipped too, with the innate longing to reach God. As St. Augustine said, "Our hearts are restless until they rest in You." Getting to the peak takes the right spiritual physique, courage to begin, willing trust and persistent effort. That's what the saints did. They weren't perfect, and it wasn't an easy journey, but they had faith in a loving God. They found the way.

A few years ago, I heard in a homily that we either have faith or we don't. It only takes faith the size of a mustard seed to get us going. We can learn, not only from the saints, but from those around us.

The question is – are we willing to reach out to step up? Are we humble enough to learn from others? Are we willing to immerse ourselves in the body of Christ? Do we have hope and faith in the ready, loving hand beckoning us from the next

ridge? I believe God provides help on the rocky path
in many ways – our job is to trust Him.

Hinds' Feet Hopes

Sure and steady on the rocky climb,
Muscled limbs with ease and grace sublime
Maneuver crags and slides with practiced steps;
Ascending heights with certitude
I've not discovered yet.

Now worn the paths that lead to Heaven's gate,
The trails marked well by saints who've gone before.
Free will is mine to journey or to wait
With seedling faith required - no less, no more.

Grant me the grace you gift to stately deer.
Make me, Your creature, tread just like the hind.
Your strength, pervade my soul and keep me near
That I may reach Your hand - Your glory find.

LEPIDOPTERA

But those who wait for the Lord shall
renew their strength, they shall mount
up with wings like eagles, they shall
run and not be weary, they shall walk
and not faint. (Isaiah 40:31)

The day after hurricane Irma, I marveled at a swallowtail butterfly gliding through my front yard; a graceful, welcome reprieve from the previous day's harsh winds. It was huge, soaring, totally unexpected. This isn't the first time a butterfly has blessed my day.

Happiness is as a Butterfly

In the early seventies, pastel posters floated around everywhere declaring,

> *Happiness is as a butterfly, which, when pursued, is always just beyond your grasp, but which, if you will sit down quietly, may alight upon you.* [4]

One of my best friends gave me a small rock with a stone butterfly atop it, because she knew how much I loved the bidding to sit quietly and coax the butterfly. I kept that rock for over forty-five years, smiling every time I remembered the person and the poster behind the gift. A few years ago, when the butterfly came unglued and was lost, I gave up the rock and replaced it with an engraving in my heart from Psalm 46:10 *"Be still and know that I am God..."* I have come to understand that He is my true happiness.

Monarch Migration

Just prior to starting fifth grade, my oldest son, Jahan, received a postcard from his teacher assigning him to research and deliver a presentation on the monarch butterfly. Monitoring my son's project yielded a great appreciation for the only butterfly known to migrate, as birds do, in winter and fly back en masse for summer. I began noticing every monarch that graced our garden, marveling at their trek, sometimes as far as three thousand miles! That such a delicate creature could survive the arduous journey amazed me. I figured this was a lesson in perseverance and trust I should remember.

More Blessings

Butterflies fight to emerge from their cocoon. Without the struggle, they don't build the strength or dryness in their wings to fly when they break free. Some years ago, I was struggling to get through the weariness of too much work, not enough time, and feelings that life would always be like this. But

God is so good. He gave me something I didn't even know I needed.

I walked out my front door one early morning, heading off to work. As I stepped from my porch, a magnificent monarch hovered in front of me, rested on a nearby bush, sipped nectar, and took flight again. I stopped and immersed myself in the present moment, thanking God for the pure beauty and joy of a simple butterfly. Then I felt peace wash over me.

Calmness remained as I realized that the battle to be free, to soar above fatigue, will always be present in an imperfect world. But along the way, the butterfly teaches us not to give up the fight to transform, to fly, even if only for a while. I thank God for the struggles that allow the breaking free and the soaring against a vast sky. The prize is winged flight and the reprieve of sweet nectar on the journey.

Lepidoptera

I long to fly
short-lived though soaring be
from embryo to crawling
then cocoon before the world I see.
Too much to bear,
the daily battle tires me.
Death sure to come, if I but pause
before emergence sets me free.

This morning, transformation is in grasp
as night skies yield to light of day
and brilliant colors spread their wings at last.
Until they fall,
Thanks for the sip to drink along the way.

MORE THAN THINGS

Blessed are the poor in spirit, for theirs is the kingdom of heaven. (Matthew 5:3)

One Sunday, the homily challenge to become "detached" convicted my ripened heart. As the priest spoke, I replayed my father's lesson on what detachment means. Daddy always sat my sisters and me down before heading to Mass to prepare us for the liturgy. He specifically told us that being poor in spirit meant that we should not be attached to possessions. Rather, we should be attached to God. The older I get, the more I understand his wisdom and gift of faith passed on.

When my children were young, I went through periods of materialism, wanting things I really didn't need, and buying them anyway. One of those things was a unique handmade bowl, by a local artisan, that was adorned with tiny blue birds. I spent a lot to purchase it, just because it was beautiful and made me smile.

One day, my young son accidentally collided with it from where it sat on my coffee table. Losing that prized possession gave me the opportunity to dig deep, in the soil of my own faith, to draw on the roots of those seeds my father planted long ago.

These days, my list of wants has to do with relationships more than things; spiritual more than material - with God at the top. I am forever grateful for parents who made passing on the faith their number one priority.

More than Things

One was my first handmade purchase -
pottery lovingly turned at the wheel,
glazed bright blue birds perched along the grey rim
waiting to sip from its wide bowl.

One was my Grandmother's
porcelain deep pink rose and black -
asymmetrical wings rising
almost as high as the flowers
meant to grace its slender vase.

Artisan labor essence - bound to the clays -
scattered in moments of unintentional mishap.
I was more shattered than the shards before me,
until memories of my father's words swept up the
pieces in his scriptured voice –
"Blessed are the poor in spirit,
 for theirs is the kingdom of heaven," my father said.
"Enjoy your treasures," my mother echoed,
  "but don't be possessed by them.
They are only things."

I comforted guileless transgressors.

DEFYING EMPTY

Peace I leave with you; my peace I give
you. I do not give to you as the world
gives. Do not let your hearts be troubled
and do not be afraid. (John 14:27)

E mptiness is a fact of life. It's not necessarily
a bad thing. An empty plate to clean means
there was food to eat. An empty sink means no
dishes to wash, and an empty mind means endless
possibilities for filling it.

Hearts and souls left empty by people, circumstances, and choices we make are another story. We must decide how we will respond to that emptiness. Sometimes, I fill it with fleeting things like food, or television, that aren't really important, like the clutter that collects on bare countertops.

There has been a rhythm and sway to the emptying and filling of my life, like the draining of a new clay pot ungrounded by soil. It overflows at the brim after a hard rain, drains, becomes empty, and fills again. It begs for rich earth and plants to take root and hold water.

I want to finally fill the clay vessel of my life with what really matters; to be grounded with the rich soil of faith and soak in the infinite waters of life in Him. I want to decrease, so that He may increase in me; to yield good fruit. And if I am empty again tomorrow, so be it. Let the hard rains and rich soil come. Lord, fill me.

Jesus said to her, "Every one who drinks of this water will thirst again, but whoever drinks of the water that I shall give him will never thirst; the water that

I shall give him will become in him a spring of water welling up to eternal life." (John 4:13-14)

Defying Empty

Empty house
Empty hole
Empty heart
Empty soul.

No more tears.
No revolution.
Unfounded fears
Without solution?

I must decrease
Breathe Him in,
With His increase -
Breathe out sin.

Empty here,
Spirit-poor, but free.
I take this cross -
Fill me.

TREASURE CUP

In this the love of God was made manifest among us, that God sent his only Son into the world, so that we might live through him. (1 John 4:9)

We are one body, united in Christ, and given the greatest treasure and blessing of all in the Holy Eucharist. As Jesus shares himself with us, He calls us to participate in the profound privilege of sharing ourselves with others, in His name, in whatever capacity He asks of us.

Years ago, I wrote a poem for my sister, Natalia. It was at a time, in her busy life, when she wondered what value her efforts produced. She was unable to see the beauty of her own example as a strong and faithful Catholic, spending time every week in Adoration, and sharing spiritual materials with all who would accept, especially her six children. Natalia was, and still is, unaware of the treasure she bestows in the example of her daily life.

When I finished the poem, I realized that it spoke, not just of my sister, but of my parents who spent their lives laying a strong faith foundation for each of their four daughters. It spoke also of my two other sisters, Mary-Frances and Virginia – in their tireless devotion to family. I realized that God places, within all of us, a treasure to be shared. God sees and it all matters.

Treasure Cup

In your selfless giving to those small moments
of each day
which drudgery or endless need or wanting
hearts require,
who can measure the cost – the price you pay
for reaching into the depths of your own
gentle soul –
past the pain, past the ache, past the weariness
to pour out love again and again?
No coin exchanged,
no accolades,
no earthly notice –
save for the hearts who one day
will reach into their own souls
to pour out love in those small moments

Let us not become weary in doing good,
for at the proper time we will reap a har-
vest if we do not give up. (Galatians 6:9)

Chapter 5:

WORLD VIEWS

Hope extends beyond our immediate sphere of life. With the availability of universal reach, through technology and rapid communication, the world is literally at our fingertips. Given such reach, the challenge to be resilient, flexible, and enduring is one that faces us every day.

> *I have said this to you, so that in me you may have peace. In the world you face persecution. But take courage; I have conquered the world! (John 16:33)*

WEEDS

Therefore, since we are surrounded by so great a cloud of witnesses, let us also lay aside every weight and the sin that clings so closely, and let us run with perseverance the race that is set before us. (Hebrews 12:1)

Years ago, I was stopped downtown by a passing train. The fairly new overpass loomed before me. Right in the middle of one large cement seam, I saw a rich, full, cluster of green weeds. I had plenty of time to consider that in nearly impossible conditions, weeds took root and grew.

I changed my mind about weeds that day. I wanted to get out of the car and tug on it to see if it would yield to pulling. I wanted to know what circumstance led it to this very place. I understood that on this earth, you can always count on weeds to persistently come back.

There is a comfort in considering weeds. They cause constant work, if you care about keeping them at bay, and yet, they have a perfect purpose in God's creation. In nature, their job has been to try and repair damaged ground, any place the soil has been "broken." Weeds evolved to be tough and hardy, able to survive in all seasons. Ancient early man ate "weeds" as crop plants.

After that day, I never pulled dandelions from my lawn, except to clip a few of their greens and test them in my salad. I purposely planted milkweed, knowing they would overtake my front walkway. Their gift greets me in the early morning, as Monarchs flutter by, when I leave for work.

That cluster of weeds remained in the overpass for a long time. It's not there today, but I am certain its offspring grows exactly where it is meant to be; exactly where the wind deposited it for someone else to draw strength from, and consider the promise of weeds.

Weeds

persistent pests
and yet
promises of enduring return.

Their dandelion wishes
scattered with each passing wind
leave behind salad-green nourishing soul sustenance,
and milkweed's sacrifice of dying pods
lures magnificent Monarchs
with its red and yellow afterbirth.

That I could pluck from the lowly weed
resilience.
Pull me through life's ploughing field
So, I can grow again, and again.

HALEEM POT

*Very truly, I tell you, unless a grain of
wheat falls into the earth and dies, it
remains just a single grain; but if it dies,
it bears much fruit. (John 12:24)*

Over ten years ago, my husband, daughter
and I visited our Iranian family in Ahwaz,
Teheran, Isfahan and Char-e Kord in the Zagros
Mountains. It was made memorable by many
occasions:

 1. My nephew's wedding,

2. A visit to Shustar and the tomb of the prophet Daniel,

3. Eating the last of summer's apricots fresh from the mountain trees,

4. Wandering through the ancient bazaar in Isfahan,

5. Visiting my niece's husband's grain factory and,

6. Visiting the first oil well in the Middle East, built in 1918 in Masjed-Soleyman (M.I.S).

But, the most precious memories of our trip come from the time spent with a loving family; small moments talking in the kitchen, cleaning greens or "sabze", eating meals at the "sofree" (a large table-cloth placed on the floor around which very large families can all sit together), dancing, laughing, and playing cards.

One of those moments happened just before dawn, when my sister-in-law, Mahin let me go with her to get the family breakfast; one of my husband's favorite meals, haleem. My daughter took a picture of us from behind, a giant woman in a chador (me) next to a petite woman (Mahin) swinging a small cauldron to be filled with "oatmeal." I lost that picture, but it is forever etched in my mind.

Mahin, like another beloved sister-in-law, Goltala, showed me women filled with unselfish, sacrificial love for their families. In their dying to self, much fruit grows.

Haleem Pot

Before light breaks the Middle Eastern skies,
before men and children rub sleep from their eyes,
before "machines" clutter dusty, pock-marked land,
she walks with black chador and haleem-pot in hand
toward the 8 x10 storefront where he has been stirring wheat,
barley and lamb broth through the night
to create a thick paste – porridge of rich and
poor alike.
His arms are strong, steeled from beating the grain
with his oar-like paddle again, and again.
She has no servant to fetch the precious
breakfast load.
Her hands are as strong as his arms;

fingers forged from bearing heavy steaming gold.

She is stronger than the round metal casing

of her pot

and for a few coins, she fills her family's bellies;

her heart filled with love is their lot.

She is not so different from the Proverbs 31 woman.

On the way home,

we are shadowed silhouettes against the dawn –

one giant cloaked figure beside her tiny form.

I take the metal cauldron to relieve her burden.

It is heavy, with a weight I never had to bear

and in my carrying, her sacrifice becomes clear.

She presents the gruel

with a tray of cinnamon, sugar and oil.

We scoop it to our mouths with hot, flat bread.

Everyone loves this meal.

Everyone loves this woman.

For a moment, I despise instant oatmeal,

as I consider the early morning and her haleem pot.

WHERE DANIEL PRAYED

All peace to you! I decree that throughout my royal domain the God of Daniel is to be reverenced and feared: For he is the living God, enduring forever; His kingdom shall not be destroyed, and his dominion shall be without end. He is a deliverer and savior, working signs and wonders in heaven and on earth, and he delivered Daniel from the lions'

*power. So, Daniel fared well during the
reign of Darius and the reign of Cyrus
the Persian. (Daniel 6:27-29)*

S tanding at the tomb of Daniel, the Prophet, in
the ancient, dusty town of Shushtar, Iran, I had
a profound experience. Across the street from the
ornate, blue-mosaic, silver-gilded mausoleum, and
plaza, stood the ruins of King Cyrus' winter palace.
Nearby was a museum with ancient stone tablets
and implements from long before the time of Christ.

Weathered stone lions caught my eye in the dis-
tance. Whether they represented the lions to which
King Darius sent Daniel is irrelevant. I was hum-
bled and awestruck at the thought of Daniel, thou-
sands of years ago, walking on the same ground.
Daniel's trust in God, amidst danger and perse-
cution, remains an inspiration. God answered his
prayers, rewarded his faith, and was pleased with
the fruit.

A rich spiritual heritage lies in that part of the
world, foreign to so many Christians today- Iraq,
home to the Tigris and Euphrates rivers, and often
thought to have been near the Garden of Eden;

modern day Turkey where the Blessed Mother lived out her life in Ephesus; and Syria where St. Paul encountered Jesus on the road to Damascus. I mention places where the Apostles spread our faith among the nations, because our Catholic/ Christian brothers and sisters are suffering severely in these places.

Martyrdom is as real now as it has been through the millennia, not just in the Middle East, but throughout the modern world. I am confident God hears the cries of his persecuted people, destined for great reward in heaven, just as he heard the prayers of Daniel facing ravenous lions.

It all seems so distant from the safety and comfort of my daily life. Would I be as brave, would I be unwavering? I only hope to stay the course, to unite now with the body of Christ, in prayer and sacrifice, to stand up daily for my faith and stand firm should that day come for me.

Until then, hope ever rises in the words of Jesus at the Sermon on the Mount,

> *Blessed are you when people revile you*
> *and persecute you and utter all kinds of*

evil against you falsely on my account.
Rejoice and be glad, for your reward is
great in heaven, for in the same way
they persecuted the prophets who were
before you. (Matthew 5: 11-12)

The fruit blossoming from Daniel's deep faith pierced the heart of a mighty king; a non-believer moved to acknowledge our living God. Might not God's children who persecute today be also moved? Let us pray then, unceasingly.

PAULA VELOSO BABADI

Where Daniel Prayed

Where Daniel prayed I stood in awe-
holy ground, ancient dust,
reverent air, silent prayer.

Where Daniel prayed I only saw
heads bowed, pilgrim vows,
hearts raised in God's praise.

Where Daniel prayed there was no war.
Palace ruins, ancient museum,
God and me and history.

Today my brothers hide in rubble-
holy ground, ancient dust,
acrid air, desperate prayer.

Aleppo and Damascus roads
once walked by Paul as faith spread,
now bear the dead
as bullets raze Christian ways.

Body of Christ wracked in pain,

trust there's reward;

deliverance claimed,

rich fruit,

the same as when Daniel prayed.

WINDOW GLIMPSES

The eye is the lamp of the body. So, if your eye is sound, your whole body will be full of light. (Matthew 6:22)

I thought, "*What am I writing and what meaning could there possibly be connecting together thoughts or sentences?*" I think God has given us all the information we need, if we have eyes to see and a heart of love to filter what comes into our view. The same could be said of knowing another person or thinking about life and beauty and our world. It all depends on the lens with which we see and the reflections coming back to us as we glimpse through the window.

I recently attended my nephew's wedding. He married a lovely young woman, and as they proclaimed wedding vows, it was apparent how deeply they love and care for one another. I gave them this poem and wished them the grace to always see each other through the lens of love, and to let the wisdom, mercy and love of the Father, Son and Holy Spirit guide them on their marriage journey. Love is what life is all about and hope is an integral part of life lived well. May you be graced with much hope thoughout the window glimpses in your life.

Window Glimpses

It's only a glimpse of
one sunbeam of light
one moment of love
one troublesome blight
one twinkling star
one glow in the morning
one wearisome sigh
one gasp of warning.
It's a thread in the tapestry
one tear on a cheek
one piece of the puzzle
one thought that I speak.

It's only a glimpse -
nose pressed to the pane-
one reflection returned
of one move in the game.
It's a portion of me,
one part of the whole
it's a glimpse through the window
to my soul.

WOMEN ARE MORE EXPENSIVE THAN MEN AND OTHER LANGUAGE LESSONS

But blessed are your eyes, for they see,
and your ears, for they hear
(Matthew 13:16)

PAULA VELOSO BABADI

A Funny Lesson

Everyone laughed. I was trying to say in Farsi, the Persian language, "Women are stronger than men," and unfortunately, it came out otherwise. "*Geruntar*" meaning "more expensive," innocently rolled off my lips instead of "*gavidtar*," or "stronger."

While chuckling along with everyone else, I hastened to explain, in English, that I meant women have great endurance. Years later, the incident reminded me that the language of the heart is always generously received by others. You see, I was just learning Farsi and trying hard, in a room full of Persians, to speak with them in their own language. Since then, with imperfect grammar and pronunciation, I now speak with relatives and friends, in broken words but with a whole heart. They never seem to mind my mistakes.

Some of the First Lessons

As a young child, I wanted to learn Tagalog, so I could speak with my Filipino grandmother when she visited. I only managed to say, "good morning"

116

and "good night." It was hard to learn from a book, with so many consonants in each word, and a dad who was out at sea most of the time, unable to help. When my grandmother visited, she was pleased with my effort, and gently corrected my inexperienced pronunciation.

When our family moved to the United States from England, I had a strong British accent amidst a deeply southern school community. I had to learn that "ya'll" meant "all of you" and that "kids" were children and not baby goats. In the language of math, I had trouble remembering that a dime was ten cents and not the same as a schilling which was fourteen cents.

My mother and father always believed in learning the language, and customs, of the country in which they lived. And Daddy always said, "*When in Rome, do as the Romans do, except in sin, of course.*" Thus, my mother learned French while we were stationed in Villefranche, just outside Nice. When my parents didn't want my sisters and I to know what they were saying at the dinner table, they spoke in French—of course.

At Barry University, in Miami, my friends from Central America patiently listened while I practiced my high school Spanish. It was often frustrating being unable to follow their rapid conversation. When I married my Iranian husband, I made extra efforts to speak slowly, and clearly, when around his friends. And they were only too happy to translate common words into their language, so I could learn.

Idioms and Accents

Words are not the only difficulty when confronted with a foreign language—accents and idioms present their own challenges. One evening while having dinner with another Iranian/American newlywed couple, some rice fell onto the shag carpet. Mansour, Leslie's husband asked her to go and get the...the...the "rug sucker" when he couldn't remember "vacuum cleaner." We all laughed. When my husband still calls his "toes," "fingers," I just smile, knowingly, as he says, "*What do you expect from a foreigner,*" and gently remind him he is no longer a foreigner after being in this country forty-seven years.

And thanks to my Dad, I understood that sometimes non-native English speakers mix up "he" and "she"; some countries have no "v" sound, so "adventure" becomes "adwenture." You get the idea.

Today, I listen carefully to people of differing languages and accents, seeking to understand and respond with interest and love. My parish has been blessed with priests from Ireland, India, Kenya, Vietnam, Poland and Brazil—each with their wonderful, unique ways of speaking. The key is they all speak that language of the heart. Their love of God, reverence for the Eucharist, and compassion for their parishioners always speak more loudly than any mispronounced words in a sermon.

Beloved, since God loved us so much, we also ought to love one another. No one has ever seen God; if we love one another, God lives in us, and his love is perfected in us. (1 John 4:11-12)

The Language that Matters

People everywhere understand the language of love. In the effort, in the trying to reach out to speak and to understand, we connect with others in a way that is beyond words. God speaks to us in a language beyond the written page in Scripture. He infuses His Spirit of understanding into those who have ears to hear, just as His Spirit guides those who proclaim His good news.

*Then how does each of us hear them in
his own native language? (Acts 2:8)*

We may never experience the magnificent fire of Pentecost, or the miraculous courage and comprehension that occurred that day, but we can experience the same Spirit. We can reach out with compassion and kindness, as we recognize language challenges for those of different heritages than our own. I am convinced that love matters, and the heart speaks and hears perfectly. God is love and when we speak His language to others, they understand.

For where your treasure is, there will be
your heart also. (Luke 12:34)

Language Lessons

Stronger than limbs
muscled by the run,
faster than heart
quickened by the race,
larger than branch
nourished by the Vine,
Love is made manifest
by this tongue of mine.

Reference List

[1] Ilibagiza, Immaculée. *Left to Tell: Discovering God Amidst the Rwandan Holocaust.* Carlsbad: *Hay House.* 2014. Print. p. 40.

[2] Gaitley, Michael E. *The One Thing is Three.* Stockbridge: *Marian Press.* 2015, First Edition (third printing) Print, p. 90.

[3] Aquinas, Thomas. *Prayer of Saint Thomas Aquinas.* Catholics Online n.d. Web. 30 Aug. 2018. **https://www.catholic.org/prayers/prayer.php?p=832**

[4] *Tender Moments*, Selected by Ben Whitley, Unnumbered page (Page 10), Kansas City: *Hallmark Editions: Hallmark Cards, Inc.,* 1971 (Copyright 1970).

About the Author

Paula Veloso Babadi loves God, her family and words. She wrote her first poem about hope when she was eight. Now, she celebrates, and shares hope grown from plowing through a lifetime of rocky fields. Paula credits her faith-filled parents for planting the seeds and thanks family, friends and even adversity for nourishing the soil.

She is board Chairperson of the St. Johns Chapter of the Catholic Writers Guild, regular contributor to St. Joseph's Reflections Magazine, and past "Poet's Voice" columnist.

Growing up in England, and Pensacola, Florida, with Filipino and British parents, and marrying into her husband's Iranian family, she now makes her home in Northeast Florida. Coupled with her culturally diverse daily life, Paula's 40-year career in healthcare, lends depth to her writing and poetry. The Babadi's have three sons, one daughter and three delightful grandchildren living close by.

Read more of her poetry at A Poet's Voice at **www.catholicstewardsofcreation.com** and **www.everywherehopetoday.org**

> *For there is hope for a tree, if it is cut down, that it will sprout again, and that its shoots will not cease. Though its root grows old in the earth, and its stump dies in the ground, yet at the scent of water it will bud and put forth branches like a young plant. (Job 14:7-9)*

Acknowledgments

E veryone who has touched my life helped write this book. My parents (Fortunato and Violet Veloso), sisters (Mary Frances, Natalia and Virginia), husband (Fatullah Jafari Babadi), children (Jahan, Daniel, Joseph, and Sheila), and extended family always provided support and inspiration. Besides family and friends, thanks to all members of the body of Christ, our Living Vine.

Special thanks to Natalie Tomola who first asked me to write for the Reflections magazine; Susi Pittman who gave me my first column on her website; Virginia Lieto, my wonderful editor; posthumously, Kathryn Cunningham, who moderated the Catholic Writers Guild (CWG) blog; all my friends and mentors from the CWG; Gerald Webster, founder of the local St. Johns Chapter; and Bishop Felipe J. Estévez, Diocese of St. Augustine, a holy shepherd and CWG encourager.

9 781545 650325